DinoZone

PLANT-EATING DINOSAURS

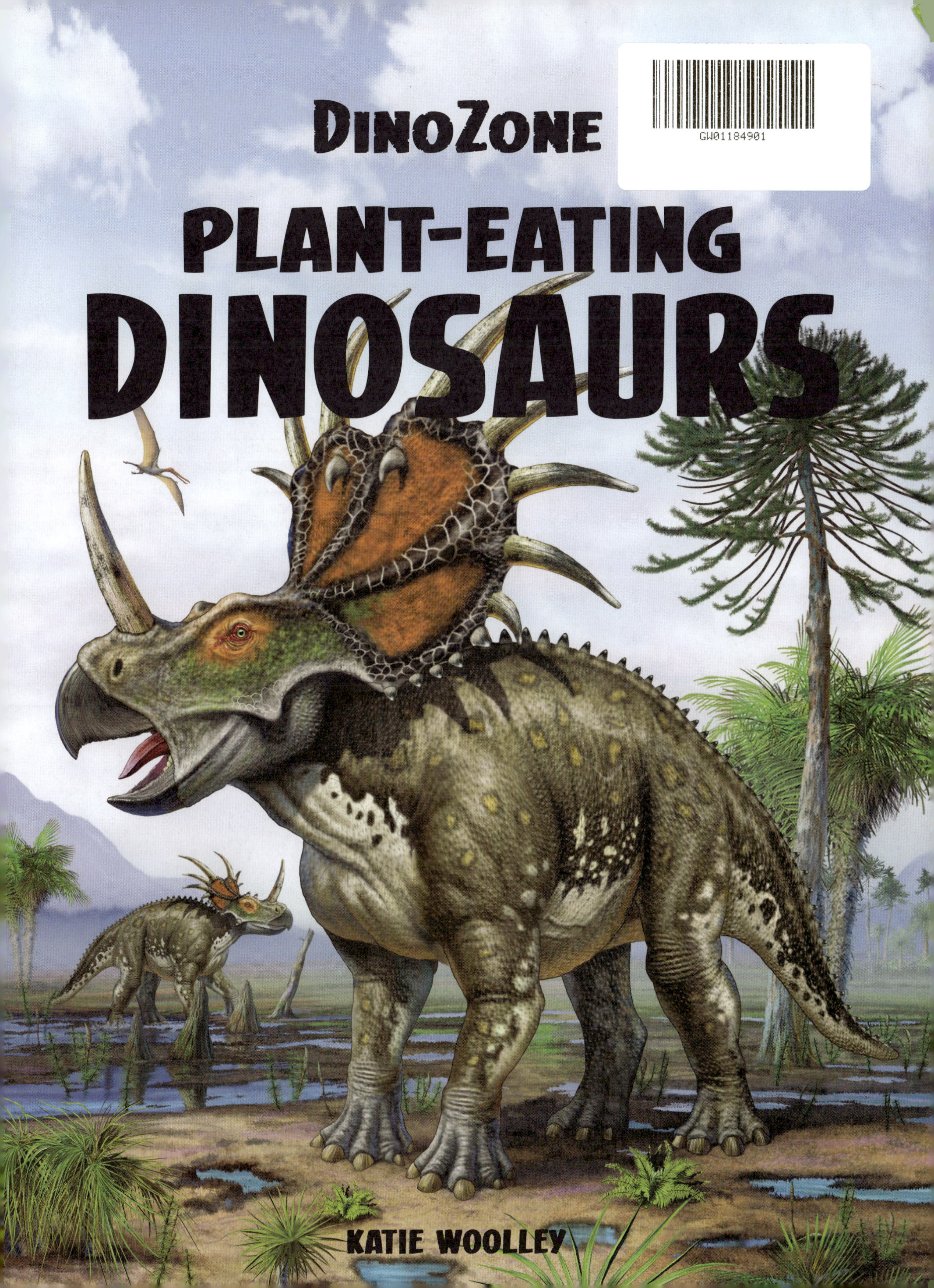

KATIE WOOLLEY

This edition published in 2020 by Arcturus Publishing Limited
26/27 Bickels Yard, 151–153 Bermondsey Street,
London SE1 3HA

Author: Katie Woolley
Designers: Neal Cobourne and Emma Randall
Editors: Joe Harris and Anna Brett

Cover illustration: Rudolf Farkas
Interior illustrations: Arcturus Image Library (Stefano Azzalin: 8, 9, 14, 15, 18, 20, 23; Martin Bustamante: 4, 7t, 10, 11, 19t, 19b, 24, 25t, 25b, 26; Juan Calle: 12, 21; Colin Howard: 14c; Kunal Kundu: 17; Jerry Pyke: 16; Parwinder Singh: 22; Val Walerczuk: 13); Wikimedia Commons: 27t; and Shutterstock: 5, 6-7, 27b, 28-29.

ISBN 978-1-83857-256-3
CH008176NT

Supplier 33, Date 1219, Print run 9715

Printed in China

CONTENTS

Peaceful plant-eaters

About two-thirds of dinosaurs were plant-eaters, or herbivores. The biggest herbivores were enormous sauropods. Some sauropods ate enough plants every day to match the weight of a small car!

Brachiosaurus (BRAH-kee-oh-SORE-us) was a sauropod that lived during the Jurassic period.
Brachiosaurus

Most plant-eaters had blunt teeth for stripping leaves from branches. Some, such as *Brachiosaurus*, walked on four legs. Others, such as *Plateosaurus* (PLAH-tee-oh-SORE-us), walked on two.

Fast Facts

Some dinosaurs swallowed rocks (gastroliths) to help break down the plants they'd eaten!

Plateosaurus was 7 m (22 ft) long.

A huge herbivore

Diplodocus (dih-PLOD-uh-KUS) was HUGE! Its tail was the longest of all the dinosaurs—as long as two tennis courts.

Diplodocus had an enormous appetite. Its peg-shaped teeth could strip the tough leaves from conifers. It also ate leaves from other plants, such as gingkos, ferns, and horsetails.

In 1905, a cast of a *Diplodocus* skeleton was given to the Natural History Museum in London, UK. Its nickname is "Dippy!"

Fast Facts

When: Late Jurassic period

Food: Leaves and soft plants

Size: 26 m (85 ft) long

Weight: 25,000 kg (27.5 tons)

How it moved: Slowly, on four legs

Found in: United States, North America

***Diplodocus* may have used its tail to whip predators!**

Spiky protector

***Stegosaurus* (STEH-goh-SORE-us) was a large, slow-moving plant-eater. It would have defended itself from predators with its powerful spiked tail.**

Fast Facts

When: Late Jurassic period

Food: Leaves and plants

Size: 9 m (30 ft) long

Weight: 3,100 kg (3.4 tons)

How it moved: Slowly, on four legs

Found in: Worldwide

Stegosaurus had 17 bony plates on its back. They may have been used to keep the dinosaur cool or to protect it from meat-eaters. Or they may have been used for impressing mates.

***Stegosaurus's* tail spikes are called a "thagomizer."**

This dinosaur had a beak, like a bird. At the back of its mouth were small teeth called "cheek teeth," which it used to chew plant leaves.

Stegosaurus means **"roof lizard."**

Three-horned threat

Triceratops **had three horns on its face. It had a bony plate called a frill at the back of its skull. A predator would have to be pretty fearless to attack this dinosaur!**

Triceratops means **"three-horned face."**

This plant-eater had a large head about 3 m (10 ft) long. That's a third of its 9-m (30-ft) length! *Triceratops* had a beak like a parrot's. Its cheek teeth helped it chew food.

***Triceratops*'s frill may have made it look more impressive.**

Triceratops probably charged at its enemy, such as other *Triceratops* or predators such as *T. rex*. It rushed with its head down and horns forward.

Fast Facts

When: Late Cretaceous period

Food: Leaves and plants

Size: 9 m (30 ft) long

Weight: 5,500 kg (6.1 tons)

How it moved: On four legs

Found in: United States, North America

Thick-headed lizard

Pachycephalosaurus **(PACK-ee-seh-fah-low-SORE-us) had a thick skull, with a dome-shaped, bony lump on top. It used this tough part of its skull to ram other dinosaurs.**

This plant-eater was probably a herd animal. Its thick skull might have been used to defend itself against predators or in mating displays.

Fast Facts

When: Late Cretaceous period

Food: Plants, fruit, and seeds

Size: 8 m (26 ft) long

Weight: 3,000 kg (3.3 tons)

How it moved: On two legs

Found in: Canada and United States, North America

Pachycephalosaurus means **"thick-headed lizard."**

Pachycephalosaurus had bumps on its snout and around the dome on its head. However, its teeth were very small. It could not have eaten tough plants.

Gentle giants

Sauropods were the biggest animals that ever walked on land. *Mamenchisaurus's* (MAH-men-kee-SORE-us) neck alone was 13 m (42.6 ft) long. Its full height would have reached the top of a building with four floors!

Sauropod means **"lizard-footed."**

Sauropods were the biggest dinosaurs. It would take a stack of three *T. rex* to reach the height of *Mamenchisaurus*!

An adult sauropod would have been too big to attack. Any predator that dared to get close enough would have been swiped by a sauropod's long tail.

Sauropods may have been big, but they had very small heads for their bodies. And they had even smaller brains! Luckily, these gentle giants didn't need to be clever.

A spiny sauropod

Amargasaurus (ah-MAR-gah-SORE-us) was a migrating dinosaur that moved in herds searching for food. This plant-eater may have eaten leaves whole, without even chewing its food before swallowing!

Fast Facts

When: Early Cretaceous period

Food: Tough plants

Size: 12 m (39 ft) long

Weight: 9,000 kg (10 tons)

How it moved: On four legs

Found in: Argentina, South America

A bizarre-looking dinosaur, *Amargasaurus* was smaller and had a shorter neck than most other sauropods. It may have looked for food on the ground, rather than up high.

The *Amargasaurus* cast in the Museums Victoria, Australia, is called "Margie."

Amargasaurus had two rows of spines along its back. These spines may have been joined by skin, so they looked like a sail. The "sail" may have been used for protection, in mating displays, or for keeping the dinosaur cool.

Amargasaurus means **"Amarga lizard."** La Amarga is a place in Argentina.

Safety in numbers

Some plant-eating dinosaurs lived in groups for protection, like zebra do today. They roamed in search of food. Some sauropods may have migrated great distances.

Herding dinosaurs could warn each other of danger. *Parasaurolophus* (PAH-rah-sore-OH-loh-fus) was especially good at this. It could make a loud noise by pushing air into the hollow crest on top of its head.

Parasaurolophus

Chasmosaurus (KAZ-moh-SORE-us)

Chasmosaurus and *Centrosaurus* probably lived in large groups. Younger animals did not have horns. They would have been protected by older members of the herd.

Centrosaurus (SEN-troh-SORE-us)

Spiky hands

***Iguanodon* (ig-WAH-no-don) was a plant-eating dinosaur that could move around on two or four legs. It had a toothless beak and cheek teeth, which it used to chew tough plants.**

This plant-eater had a bendy little finger for grasping food and sharp thumb claws for prying open tough fruits. The claws also protected it against predators.

Fast Facts

When: Early Cretaceous period

Food: Plants

Size: 10 m (33 ft) long

Weight: 4,000 kg (4.4 tons)

How it moved: On two or four legs

Found: Worldwide

Iguanodon means **"iguana tooth."**

Scientists used to think that *Iguanodon's* thumb claws were horns!

Iguanodon lived during the Cretaceous period when Pangaea was breaking up into many continents. Fossils of this dinosaur have been found in North America, Europe, and Asia.

A living tank

***Ankylosaurus* (AN-kuh-loh-SORE-us) was a big, heavy plant-eater that moved slowly. Because of its large size, it needed to eat a lot of plants to stay alive!**

Ankylosaurus had short legs, so it walked fairly low to the ground. Its narrow beak and small teeth helped it strip leaves from low-lying plants.

***Ankylosaurus* could attack predators with the bony club at the end of its tail.**

Fast Facts

When: Late Cretaceous period

Food: Plants

Size: 7 m (23 ft) long

Weight: 4,000–7,000 kg (4.4–7.7 tons)

How it moved: On four legs

Found in: Canada and United States, North America

This dinosaur is possibly the most heavily protected dinosaur we know about. Its body was covered in thick bony plates, two rows of spikes, large horns, and a tail like a club. Its plates were probably made from keratin—the same stuff as your fingernails!

Ankylosaurus means **"stiff lizard."**

Dinosaur defenders

Scientists think that many plant-eaters had tough, leathery skin. This was to protect them from the razor-sharp teeth of meat-eating dinosaurs. But many had other weapons they could use in an attack.

Size was a big help! Only ferocious predators or pack hunters would try to kill a mighty sauropod such as *Titanosaurus* (TIE-tan-oh-SORE-us). Others, such as *Tuojiangosaurus* (too-YANG-oh-sore-us) and *Styracosaurus* (sty-RAH-koh-SORE-us), protected themselves with horns, bony plates, and spikes.

Styracosaurus

Camouflage markings may have helped plant-eating dinosaurs blend into their surroundings. This way, hungry predators might not see them.

Mother *Maiasaura*

A fantastic fossil find in North America revealed a *Maiasaura* (my-ah-SORE-ah) nesting site. *Maiasaura* mothers laid their eggs in a circle and covered them with earth and leaves to keep them safe and warm.

Maiasaura lived in herds to protect themselves from predators like *Troodon*. This is also why females laid their eggs together, so there was more than one adult to keep watch over the nests and young.

Maiasaura eggs were oval and around 15 cm (6 in) long.

Maiasaura laid up to 30 eggs at a time in one nest. Once the eggs hatched, the young were at risk of attack, and they had to quickly learn how to fend for themselves.

Fast Facts

When: Late Cretaceous period

Food: Leaves and plants

Size: 9 m (29.5 ft) long

Weight: 2,500 kg (2.7 tons)

How it moved: On two or four legs

Found in: United States, North America

Maiasaura means **"good mother reptile."**

Fossils around the world

Plant-eating dinosaurs lived all over the world. We know this because of where their fossils have been found. Can you see a plant-eater that would have existed near you?

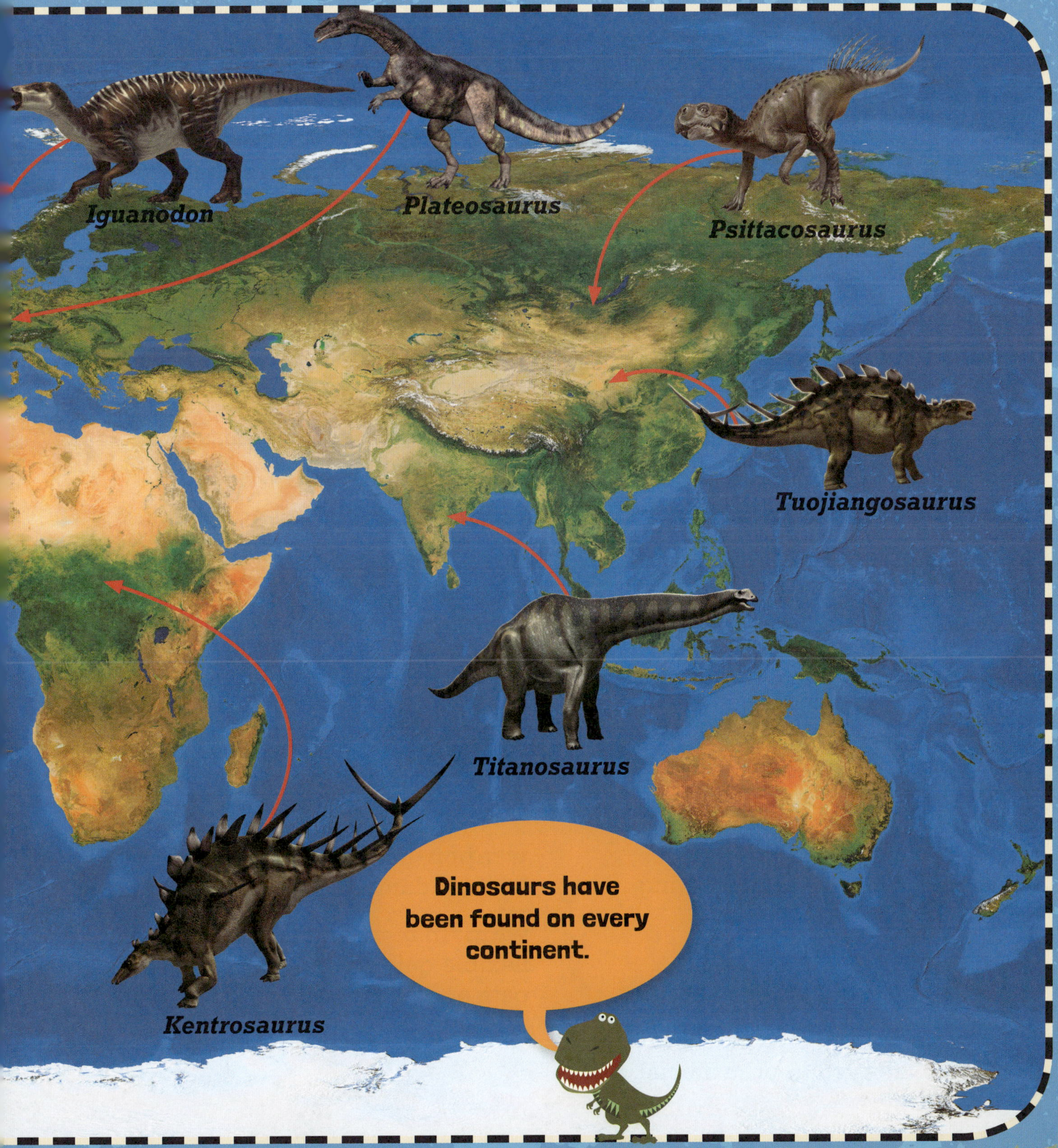

Glossary

appetite A desire to eat food.

camouflage The appearance of an animal that helps it to blend in with its surroundings.

charge To move forward quickly as an attack.

continent A very large area of land, mostly or completely surrounded by water. Modern Earth has seven continents.

Cretaceous period A period in Earth's history, between 144 and 65 million years ago.

fearless Not having any fear.

ferocious Fierce, violent, or aggressive.

fossil The remains or imprint of an animal or plant, preserved for millions of years, now turned to stone.

gastrolith A rock swallowed by a dinosaur to help break down tough plant material in its stomach.

grasp Grab and hold strongly.

herd A group of animals living together.

Jurassic period A time in Earth's history, between 206 and 144 million years ago.

mate The partner of an animal.

migrate To move from one place to another to find more food or better conditions.

nest A place chosen or made by an animal in which to lay its eggs.

oval A shape like a stretched circle.

Pangaea One vast area of land on Earth that existed before it broke up into separate continents.

predator An animal that eats other animals.

ram Crash violently against something else.

roam Move about a large area of land.

sauropods Large plant-eating dinosaurs with long necks and tails.

skeleton A frame made up of all the bones in an animal's body.

Triassic period A period in Earth's history between 248 and 206 million years ago.

weapon Something used to cause harm or damage.

whip To move something long and flexible quickly, in order to cause pain or damage.

Further information

Further reading

The Complete Book of Dinosaurs by Dougal Dixon (Southwater, 2012)

Dinosaur Encyclopedia by Caroline Bingham (DK Children's, 2009)

Jurassic Record Breakers by Darren Naish (Carlton Kids, 2015)

National Geographic Little Kids First Big Book of Dinosaurs by Catherine D. Hughes (National Geographic Children's Books, 2011)

Planet Dinosaur by editors of the BBC (BBC Books, 2011)

Websites

www.enchantedlearning.com/subjects/dinosaurs
Dinosaur information pages, fact sheets, and printouts, as well as a list of famous paleontologists.

www.thedinosaurmuseum.com/dino-facts
Facts about record-breaking dinosaurs, including the heaviest, smallest, and oldest. You can also print out dinosaur pictures to shade in.

Index